INFLUENCER
FAST START

21
PROVEN STRATEGIES
FOR BUILDING
YOUR
PERSONAL BRAND

Dan Kirkmann

Table of Contents

INTRODUCTION 5
CHAPTER 1 8
    WHAT IS A PERSONAL BRAND? 8
CHAPTER 2 12
    BENEFITS OF CREATING YOUR PERSONAL BRAND 12
CHAPTER 3 16
    WHY YOU NEED A PERSONAL BRAND? 16
CHAPTER 4 19
    STRATEGY 1 - BUILD YOUR PERSONAL BRAND WITH ATTRACTION MARKETING 19
CHAPTER 5 22
    STRATEGY 2 – BUILD YOUR PERSONAL BRAND WITH BLOGS 22
CHAPTER 6 26
    STRATEGY 3 – BUILD YOUR PERSONAL BRAND WITH PUBLIC RELATIONS 26
CHAPTER 7 30
    STRATEGY 4 – BUILD YOUR PERSONAL BRAND WITH ONLINE VIDEO MARKETING 30
CHAPTER 8 34
    STRATEGY 5 – BUILD YOUR PERSONAL BRAND WITH ARTICLE MARKETING 34
CHAPTER 9 37
    STRATEGY 6 – BUILD YOUR PERSONAL BRAND WITH BRANDING BY ASSOCIATION 37

CHAPTER 10 39
  STRATEGY 7 – BUILD YOUR PERSONAL BRAND WITH INBOUND MARKETING CAMPAIGN 39
CHAPTER 11 44
  STRATEGY 8 – BUILD YOUR PERSONAL BRAND WITH TWITTER 44
CHAPTER 12 47
  STRATEGY 9 - BUILD YOUR PERSONAL BRAND BY MASTERING CONSISTENCY 47
CHAPTER 13 52
  STRATEGY 10 – BUILD YOUR PERSONAL BRAND WITH FACEBOOK 52
CHAPTER 14 58
  STRATEGY 11 – BUILD YOUR PERSONAL BRAND WITH BOOK PUBLISHING 58
CHAPTER 15 62
  STRATEGY 12- BUILD YOUR PERSONAL BRAND WITH PERSEVEARNCE 62
CHAPTER 16 65
  STRATEGY 13 – BUILD YOUR PERSONAL BRAND WITH INTEGRITY 65
CHAPTER 17 69
  STRATEGY 14 – BUILD YOUR PERSONAL BRAND WITH CREDIBILITY 69
CHAPTER 18 73
  STRATEGY 15 – BUILD YOUR PERSONAL BRAND WITH CUSTOM PROMOTIONAL PRODUCT 73
CHAPTER 19 76
  STRATEGY 16 – BUILD YOUR PERSONAL BRAND WITH YOUTUBE CHANNEL 76

- CHAPTER 20 80
  - STRATEGY 17 – BUILD YOUR PERSONAL BRAND WITH JOINT VENTURE 80
- CHAPTER 21 83
  - STRATEGY 18 – BUILD YOUR PERSONAL BRAND WITH WEB DESIGN 83
- CHAPTER 22 86
  - STRATEGY 19 - BUILD YOUR PERSONAL BRAND WITH PHOTO KEY RINGS 86
- CHAPTER 23 89
  - STRATEGY 20 – BUILD YOUR PERSONAL BRAND WITH BRAND BOOK 89
- CHAPTER 24 95
  - STRATEGY 21 – A BUILD YOUR PERSONAL BRAND WITH AFFILIATE MARKETING 95
- CHAPTER 25 98
  - TIPS FOR A SUCCESSFUL PERSONAL BRANDING STRATEGY 98
- CONCLUSION 105

INTRODUCTION

Personal branding describes the process by which individuals, usually entrepreneurs, differentiate themselves and stand out from competitors by identifying and communicating what makes them unique.

Similar to that of product branding, personal branding is a way to enhance recognition. You become a brand.

You can leverage your brand by carrying a consistent message and image in your marketing strategy, regardless of the product or business venture you undertake. In this way, you can enhance your recognition as an expert in your field, establish reputation and credibility, and build self-confidence.

A sound personal branding campaign creates a strong and consistent association between the individual and their perceived value. Personal branding is especially common among entertainment, political, and sports figures. In business, individuals such as Donald Trump have created enormous visibility and success by actively promoting their personal brands.

For example, regardless of whether it is on Donald Trump's reality show or another one of his successful ventures or investments, you know that Donald Trump will show you how to become successful.

It is not just the knowledge that you know his business will be successful. His branding supersedes his business, he is seen as a person that is successful and therefore has a perceived value that will in turn make you successful.

Your customers also need you to be seen as a person that is successful and has a perceived value that will, in turn, make them successful. In essence they are investing as much in YOU as they are in your product or service.

It is therefore important to sell yourself and earn their trust and respect, so that your image, your perceived value, carries from one business to the next.

Personal branding typically begins with identifying your core competencies and values. What are your areas of expertise? What abilities do you demonstrate? What do you stand for? What is important to you? What makes you different than others?

Once you identify your skills and values, in order to brand yourself, you need to make a resolute effort to focus on and manage your reputation by executing your core competencies and values in all that you do.

This branding will help you with your networking efforts as well, allowing you build important relationships with people who trust you so that you can then use this network as a resource for new business opportunities.

As your reputation builds, your personal brand will shine through every business venture you are involved in today, and in the future.

This influencer starter guide will enlighten you more about personal branding and 21 smart strategies to start building your personal brand today.

Happy Reading.

CHAPTER 1

WHAT IS A PERSONAL BRAND?

Personal branding represents a powerful personal self-promotion and small business strategy. You create a Personal Brand based on your talents, skills and values.

This Personal Brand identity becomes the foundation for all your marketing efforts. With a clear marketing identity, you can intentionally shape positive perceptions about you - as the symbol for your company.

Think about brands you use and recognize. Your perceptions about those brands have been shaped by consistent and persistent marketing messages. When your personal experience as a customer confirms those messages, the brand perception becomes reality.

Do you know any small businesses with a strong brand identity?

One of the most powerful small business owners tools is personal branding. Examples of individuals who created strong Personal Brands and developed them into multi-million-dollar enterprises include Oprah Winfrey, Martha Stewart, Nora Roberts, Stephen Covey, Tiger Woods and Tommy Hilfiger.

However, very few small business owners will use branding to be distinctive from their competitors. You are likely to be aware of a business owner with a strong personal brand only if they are active in your market space or network.

Most small business owners just don't know how and won't make the effort to use personal brand reputation building as an effective marketing strategy.

In the world today, there are two distinct groups of people, those who understand the power of personal branding and apply it to all facets of their lives, and those who aren't even aware of its existence as a force impacting on their lives on a minute by minute level.

So what is this phenomenon of personal branding?

Is it real?

Or another of the plethora of modern clichés stolen

from the marketing world and adapted to other uses. At Synergy, we tend to see personal branding as being real, only in as much as a brand in its commercial sense, is an entity with unique positioning in the mind of the consumer, so a person is much the same.

Think of anyone you know and write down the tangible attributes that make that person unique to you and distinctly separate to the other people you know. Just as a brand, such as Coke or Persil may have a physical size, color and weight, so there are the human equivalent visible attributes, clothing hair color, height and build etc.

Then think about the elements of the person that are perhaps not as immediately apparent, this may be their disposition, character, experience, sense of humor, you get the idea.

Marketers take these elements and create a 'brand iceberg' this is simply the attributes that are visible, the top part of the iceberg, combined with the non-visible qualities, the hidden part of the iceberg.

The interesting part of personal branding is that if marketers can cleverly manipulate the perceptual elements of a brand so we build a preference for that brand over that of its competition, so it enters our 'evoked set' the brands we like and trust. Then can we alter perception on a personal basis so we are perceived differently, getting more buy-in to us?

The answer to this is positively a yes. We are all familiar with how we adapt our personal appearance to create an appropriate look for individual situations such as a wedding, a night out or a job interview.

We are altering our physical presence to be perceived in a certain way appropriate to that situation and we do it without consciously thinking in terms of it being our personal branding.

Personal branding is applying a little more attention to the areas of your appearance, attitude and demeanor that interface with other people. In learning in a detailed way how we are likely to be perceived and then altering certain attributes within our 'brand architecture' we can create a totally different impression of ourselves.

CHAPTER 2

BENEFITS OF CREATING YOUR PERSONAL BRAND

For some, the idea of a personal brand is new. Some might think that they don't want to "be a brand." Others might think that branding is not for them (it's for celebrities). Some might even think that building a personal brand requires a team of professionals working around the clock.

But it's not something you complete in a few days, weeks, or months. In fact you might have to wait for its benefits over the longer term. It is, however, so important to build your brand in today's social context, particularly when you want to differentiate yourself from others.

Building a brand is not as complicated as it you might think. Your personal brand is a culmination of sharing your expertise, your experiences, showcasing your achievements, getting your due recognition, building trusted connections, and continuously marketing your strengths. That's all it is.

Take control of your professional career and get serious about a personal branding strategy. Here are five benefits that make it worth your time:

1. Show Your Uniqueness

Investing time and effort in your personal brand is crucial to your success. If you are asking, "What's in it for me?" You should know that the most important element of a personal brand is that it differentiates you from others who haven't invested resources in developing an online presence. Stand out from the crowd. Carve out your niche.

After all, there is no competition for the inimitable you. Your brand can reflect some of the best of what you would like to show the world.

Your brand can be staged on a platform where your digital reputation, professional experience, and portfolio come together and lend credibility the way you market yourself. It can serve as a dynamic business card and be even more valuable than one when people seek you out.

2. Control Public Perception

Branding is about how you are perceived in the market, and today you have control over that. Personal brand management is about cultivating the pieces that tell your story. You can build a great reputation with your willingness to share knowledge and expertise. In today's socially connected world, your reputation can have global reach.

This makes your brand more important than ever. Social media has given us an opportunity like never before to communicate with others. It also allows us to shape our brand with a myriad of online tools. You can proactively protect and maintain your public image by investing time in your brand.

3. Build a Following

Each social media outlet offers you the opportunity to build a following. You can become known as an expert in your profession by focusing your effort, planning, and generously sharing your time. But, before putting in your time, make sure you establish your goal in building a following. In other words, "What is your objective in building a following"?

4. Leverage your brand

When you invest time in building your personal brand, you can leverage it to reach valuable connections, find the right avenues for business or career, and secure a high level of visibility. Your brand can be the gateway to your entrepreneurial pursuits and passions. Imagine your brand as leverage in building professional equity.

5. Learn From Your Connections

Branding helps your connections and audience to understand who you are. It also helps you project your value proposition. Interested parties can reach out to you for just about anything. You, in turn, can reach out to them.

This is how you build a network of connection that you can learn from and to whom you can contribute. This is how you create circles of trust. It may take time and effort to cultivate relationships like these, but once established, with your continued nurture, no one can take away what you've sown.

CHAPTER 3

WHY YOU NEED A PERSONAL BRAND?

Successful people know and express who they are. They have honed and communicated their professional identity and made others aware of their personal attributes - their expertise, talents, and deepest commitments. In other words, these people have developed a personal brand - or a "Brand You," the term coined by Tom Peters.

Mention their names, and you instantly think of a set of personal attributes, in much the same way we might associate attributes such as "reliable, fuel-efficient, and low-maintenance" with a certain brand of car. However, a personal brand is not a superficial marketing ploy.

It is as different from a product brand as a dynamic, complex person is from an inanimate object. "Brand You" emerges from a person's deepest commitments, interests, and unique "genius." What are some famous personal brands?

Bill Gates: Technology genius: Harvard dropout who founded Microsoft to become the world's richest man. Philanthropist: Puts his wealth to work in huge global projects for the public good.

Oprah Winfrey: Brilliant entrepreneur: Billionaire talk-show TV personality and media owner. Social pioneer: As a black woman, overcame racial and gender barriers to be embraced by households of every race and ethnicity in 12 countries.

Warren Buffett: Stock market investment genius: Financial oracle known for being right about achieving investment gains in both up and down markets and amassing huge wealth. New image of "rich": Buffett lives frugally compared to most of the "rich and famous."

What is the value of a personal brand? Whether you're a celebrity or just a knowledgeable, mature worker with years of valuable experience, establishing a clear and authentic personal brand can bring multiple benefits. It allows you to:

Control the direction of your career by increasing your

visibility and ability to attract and land target jobs.

You'll spend less time and money on job searches and personal marketing because your brand will do a lot of the selling for you (online, offline and wherever you go).

Request and receive higher compensation for your work because your offerings are unique and differentiated in your market.

Experience personal fulfillment by aligning your career with your authentic self.

Conversely, without a strong personal brand, you may miss out on key business and career opportunities.

In the next few chapters, I'll be explaining 21 effective strategies for building your personal brand. I hope you will make the best use of them. Read on.

CHAPTER 4

STRATEGY 1 - BUILD YOUR PERSONAL BRAND WITH ATTRACTION MARKETING

The way business works has changed drastically over the past few years. The mindset of the "salesperson" desperately trying to convince potential customers to read their material and buy their product is almost dead. The new way to do online business has to do with Attraction Marketing.

Attraction marketing principles show us that it is time to turn the tables and have the customer chasing you. How are you going to make that happen? Is this even possible? Well, it's all about how you set your business up and what marketing strategies you use to attract clients and partners.

Attraction marketing principles showcase an important step to getting potential clients and partners to sign up for your business venture:

Personal Branding. This is all about making people out there realize that you are not part of the herd. You are different.

What you are offering is useful and you want to share it with the world. By showing the world who you are and the valuable things you have to offer, you can expect to build a long-lasting and successful business.

Personal Branding is accomplished by letting the world get to know more about you. This can be done through videos, pictures, blogs, interviews, web pages and other publicity and PR campaigns.

Personal Branding can be accomplished with an effective publicity and promotion strategy where people feel you are talking to them, but not trying to push your product on them.

By becoming an expert in your field and branding your knowledge, you get people to let go of their loathing for the salesperson. That's not who you are. You aren't selling anything; you're just trying to help.

When people see you are genuinely interested in getting to know them and finding out what they really need, the will be more likely to sign up for your business venture. People don't sign up to generic web sites; they want to feel they are joining a club with real people - like you.

Attraction marketing principles are centered on the social nature of human beings. We don't like to be alone. We don't really get along with automated systems. We want to communicate with other people. We are always on the lookout for a learning opportunity. With attraction marketing, customers look for providers. Not the other way around.

Through Personal Branding, you will become the expert in your niche. People will get to know you as a prominent figure in your desired area of expertise and others will want to get in touch with you. They'll want to learn from you.

They will be attracted to your business and your product, and the chase will be over. The days of calling up all your friends and family to rally up support for your new business venture are over. With your new found expert status, you will be able to sit back and wait for the potential clients to contact you.

CHAPTER 5

STRATEGY 2 – BUILD YOUR PERSONAL BRAND WITH BLOGS

There are many strategies we can use to ensure that we are "virtually visible" and one of the most effective and low cost strategies for building your personal brand online is the authoring of your own business blog.

But what if you do not have a business blog yourself?

How can you use business blogging as a strategy to build your personal brand online?

Well, have you noticed that most business blogs invite comments? The reason for this is that the business blogger who is the author of that blog are looking to build a community online and encourage dialogue and conversation amongst their readers.

Commenting on someone's business blog, expressing your expertise and personal brand can attract more potential clients to come and find out about you. You see most business bloggers will take notice of the comments that are added to their blog. Both the blogger and their visitors will very often check the link to see who the person is that made the comment.

YOUR PERSONAL BRAND ACTION STEP:

Why not find 30 minutes this week to take time to make valuable contributions in your field of expertise to a highly respected and trafficked business blog?

You just never know who might be reading that blog and who just may be looking for expertise like yours.

As a blogger personal branding is one of the most important strategies you can take to help establish your site. Most popular blogs have become so because they built their reputation around certain unique characteristics.

In fact the use of identity branding is a commonly used strategy to help increase blog traffic. When you think about it there is really no easier way to distinguish your blog from the millions that can be found on the internet today.

Here are 3 advantages you can expect to enjoy by

establishing your own personal brand when bogging on the internet.

Sets You Apart

Even if the topic you blog about is similar to that of other sites your insight makes it completely different. Even the most popular blogs contain information that can be found elsewhere, it is just their 'spin' on the issues that makes it unique.

No matter what your personality is or your opinions may be there will always be people who agree with you or will be attracted to your style. The best way to increase blog traffic is always to step away from the 'pack' and be the individual that you are. In this way it is more likely you will create some sort of stir or interest.

Encourages Your Individuality

You are always more comfortable in your 'own skin' and this makes the blogging 'process' all the easier for you.

The result here is that the content you produce tends to be increasingly more unique as you shed your inhibitions about sharing perspectives or making suggestions. This is all part of the identity branding process and your blog is actually 'maturing' as it takes on and grows into its personality.

Stimulates Creative Juices

Once you have hit your 'comfort zone' you now feel more comfortable about tackling issues with which you may have an opinion or even suggest solutions.

Everybody has pet peeves or personal passions as you likely also do and now you can pursue them from the 'pulpit' which is your blog. With your personal brand already established your readers now know what to expect and this is likely why they continue to return.

In fact most popular blogs use identity branding like this in the same way to gain their success online as well. The 3 advantages we reviewed here are strong reasons as to why you should establish your own personal brand.

Blogs are meant to be unique and since this is what appeals to readers it only makes sense to allow your site to be an extension of your own unique personality.

CHAPTER 6

STRATEGY 3 – BUILD YOUR PERSONAL BRAND WITH PUBLIC RELATIONS

A Public Relations strategy is carefully considered and strategically created to communicate the right message to the right audience in the right way.

In today's world, publicity is everything. If you own a company, you should have a Big vision to accomplish and a PR Agency who could understand your Vision to act upon.

PR builds strategies on how to perform effectively and efficiently in promoting a Brand, establish their target market, work on different news angles, to create a story that convince media to cover and attract the attention of Target Audiences.

PR encompasses several Branding activities that are designed to improve relationships with audiences that matter to Business Growth and Success. Richard Branson, who is a famous business magnate, investor and philanthropist has once said, "Publicity is absolutely critical. A good PR story is infinitely more effective than a front page ad."

Thus PR is always result-oriented and a winning throw, if your agency understands your company's key message and of course the Market Analysis.

The reasons why we should believe in the power of Public Relations:

Public Relations can be proved as a good investment in terms of ROI, and then other marketing tools. If PR campaign is managed well it can create three times as many leads through its specialty of content marketing and Media Relations.

By promoting, engaging content, a brand gets recognized as a market leader along with the effective use of PR tools like opinion pieces and expert views, they position company's spokespeople as experts in their fields, bringing attention towards the brand.

Increased visibility through blog posts, radio spots, articles, interviews and editorials makes target market more aware and allows a brand to showcase its importance.

Public Relations influences the opinion of target market, and can reach towards your audiences using voices they trust, with a careful selection of influencers based on your brand image. From Media Exposure to events, to websites and social media channels, PR gets your brand as close to your audience as possible.

PR agencies, as opposed to advertising agencies, promote companies or individuals via editorial coverage. This is known as "earned" or "free" media i.e. stories appearing on websites, newspapers, magazines and TV programs are more influential and effective as compared to "paid media" or advertisements.

PR agencies and advertising agencies share the same goals; promoting clients in all possible dimensions. But the strategy differs as PR plays with their skills and Innovative Strategies whereas, Advertising is a paid source.

When a company advertises, people are assured they will speak well about themselves. But when a company goes for PR Activities, media speaks about the company, thus PR is like making someone talk good about your company.

The person responsible for PR, executes various methods to attract the attention and interest so as to develop positive expectations in the minds of the public.

In turn, this method and skill of creating and maintaining brand loyalty with PR methods is "a perfect marketing storm," This tells how PR management carefully seeks to support a brand's identity in the hearts and minds of consumers.

Public Relations have been considered a vital component for building brand value, maintaining brand vitality and establishing brand credibility.

CHAPTER 7

STRATEGY 4 – BUILD YOUR PERSONAL BRAND WITH ONLINE VIDEO MARKETING

Online video marketing is an excellent way to brand yourself and your online business. If you are an online marketer and you are having difficulties finding success then maybe you need to take a look at how you are marketing your business and more importantly ask yourself the question, are you using online video as one of your marketing strategies?

By implementing online video into your online marketing strategy your prospects will get to know you, trust you and respect you therefore making it easier for you to build a relationship with them. When they click the play button it will feel like you are talking directly to them allowing you to connect with them on a much deeper level.

If you interact with them in this way and give them

priceless information that will assist them in their own business they will begin to see you as a leader in your field and in turn be more inclined to do business with you.

If for example you are a network marketer, rather than being like the majority of marketers in your business who are using company replicated websites to send prospects to, it would be a good idea for you to be different and produce your own websites and squeeze pages that include your own personal video message.

Otherwise when someone searches for your network marketing company they won't be able to find you amongst the countless other sites that are exactly like yours.

If yours is distinctive and has your own style including your personal video message, then people will be attracted to you and you will have a greater likelihood of funneling more prospective customers into your business. It seems easy enough right? But so many folk are not doing it.

The secret is to find tools that will allow you generate a buzz and add the wow factor to your marketing efforts. You need to create a unique brand around yourself and your business and online video marketing is the answer. If you follow any of the biggest internet marketers you will be aware that they are all branding themselves in this way.

I know that for some people just the thought of getting in front of a video camera and recording a video is quite scary but for anyone who is serious about having success online it is vital that they find a way to brand themselves using video.

Once you have made a couple of video's it soon gets easier and with practice it becomes a lot of fun to make them.

YouTube is fantastic for getting your videos viewed but the down side is that there are other videos on there and you can end up unknowingly sending your potential customers to your competitors.

YouTube also consists of distracting ads that are unrelated to your business again causing the person you sent to see your video to become distracted from your offer.

There are some reputable company's offering

marketers their own personal video driven websites where you can showcase yourself, your business or anything you like so do your due diligence and find one that suits you.

CHAPTER 8

STRATEGY 5 – BUILD YOUR PERSONAL BRAND WITH ARTICLE MARKETING

There are a thousand ways that article marketing will promote your personal brand, some more obvious than some. While article marketing does promote your personal brand by driving traffic to your website and by getting your name to the masses, there are also some more subtle ways that article marketing can promote your personal brand.

That's by making customers feel secure in you and your brand. And that makes them more apt to buy from you than from one of your competitors.

Article marketing, when done properly, brings customers informative and helpful information - for free. In a day and age when everything comes with a price, that's very valuable. When customers read the information, and see your personal brand attached to it, you automatically become the expert on the subject.

They feel as though they can go to you for any product, or with any issue, and that you'll be able to help them. And if you're willing to provide so much information for free, think of the benefits they'll get when they start doing business with you.

Personal branding is important specifically for the purpose of building brand loyalty and a loyal customer following. And that's exactly what customer security is all about - making the customer feel comfortable enough with one brand or one company that they feel secure enough to continue to use that company.

Article marketing not only draws people in at first, with the secure knowledge that you're an expert, but it also builds a loyal customer base and has those same customers coming back for years because they now feel completely secure doing business with you.

Attaching your name to helpful information, that's available to anyone free of charge, is one of the more subtle ways that article marketing can promote your personal brand. But it's also one of the best.

After you've given people all the information you can about how to care for something, or what you need to look for when buying something, they'll know that you truly want them to receive exactly what it is they need, and that you're the expert that can help them get it.

They read your articles, find your information helpful, and become familiar with you and your name. When the time comes that they need that product or service you're likely going to be one of the first companies they call. Nothing is more important than customer security in a world full of competition, and article marketing to promote your brand will help you get it.

CHAPTER 9

STRATEGY 6 – BUILD YOUR PERSONAL BRAND WITH BRANDING BY ASSOCIATION

Branding by association is the process of strategically positioning yourself through relationships with well-known and highly successful experts or brands. And, the really good news is that you do not have to personally know the expert to enact this strategy.

Following are five steps you can take immediately to begin implementing you own branding by association strategy:

Research and identify five to seven brands or experts who are in contact with your ideal prospects and clients. And, from whom your clients are already purchasing products.

Select three to five of those brands or experts with whom you would like to be associated. The key here is to select experts who have a reputation that could positively impact your brand.

Identify three places in which you can provide helpful information to their prospects and clients. Think blogging comments, forum interaction and social media posts.

Identify three ways to promote these brands and experts to your prospects, clients and community. This could include links to their blogs, re-tweeting their comments, and reviewing and promoting their products on an affiliate basis.

Establish a system to make these interactions part of your daily business activities. They do not have to take a great deal of time. On the contrary, this strategy can be implemented in fewer than 30 minutes per day.

Branding by association is one of the strategies that can provide a halo effect for your business by connecting and building relationships with other successful entrepreneurs.

CHAPTER 10

STRATEGY 7 – BUILD YOUR PERSONAL BRAND WITH INBOUND MARKETING CAMPAIGN

Inbound marketing, also known as content marketing, is a concept that has been popularized by the Internet because it is a marketing strategy that magnetizes customers to you, rather than forcing your sales message out to them.

A successful campaign would result with your website to ranking high in Google and other search engine results, generate buzz and engagement through social media, and attracts warm leads to your website by offering valuable content like free resources and tools, rather than having to resort to traditional outbound marketing techniques such paid advertisements.

Here are 5 steps to creating a successful inbound marketing campaign to enhance your personal branding and brand strategy efforts.

1. Employ Proper On-Page Search Engine Optimization (SEO)

The first step to building your brand through successful inbound marketing is ensuring that your website is properly search engine optimized. If you're going to attract customers naturally, also known as creating organic traffic, you're going to need to make sure that Google and other search engines are ranking you highly for your keywords.

When focusing on keywords relating to your brand, ensure that they are located within your domain name, the titles of your pages and blog posts, and in the body of your content with a moderate density.

By using proper keyword placement and providing your visitors with unique content, you will push up your website and web pages within search results. When someone types in one of your keywords, you want your site to be what comes up on the first page of search results, preferably in the #1 spot.

Keep in mind that there is more to earning a high-ranking than just on-page SEO, but this is the foundation for the rest of your brand strategy efforts.

2. Use Anchor Text Links

Anchor text is simply a link containing your chosen keywords. This makes the link more powerful and provides a positive effect on your personal branding since you will be closely associated with those keywords.

While anchor text links are typically used as a form of off-page SEO involving back links, they can also be a very powerful part of your inbound marketing strategy within your own site by directing visitors to special offers, relevant information or to a landing page.

3. Provide Strong Calls to Action

This inbound marketing strategy goes hand in hand with anchor links. If you want your visitors to do something, you can't be passive about it. You must give them clear instructions and tell them exactly what to do. This is a very basic form of copywriting, but it works wonders for conversions, if done correctly.

If you're selling something, use calls to action like "Click Here to Get Your Free E-Book Today." or

"Don't Wait. This Offer Won't Last Forever. Click Here NOW." A strong call to action gives clear instructions, instills a sense of urgency and gives your visitors an enticing reason to click your links.

4. Hire a Copywriter

Developing an inbound marketing campaign can be time consuming for even the most experienced writer. Consider hiring a professional copywriter. Copywriters have developed the skill of getting readers to act using the written word and can help to shape visitors' thoughts, perceptions and emotions to present your brand in a positive way.

In the print world, hiring a copywriter can cost thousands of dollars. The good news is that, on the Internet, you often can find copywriters for much cheaper at sites like Fiverr, Guru or Upwork for Hire section of the Warrior Forum. When you hire a copywriter, ensure that they understand your personal branding strategy thoroughly before they begin writing content for your inbound marketing campaign.

5. Use Social Media

Sites like Facebook, Twitter and Digg are extremely popular and are more than just a way to form social groups. Incorporating social media into your inbound marketing campaign will not only help generate traffic to your website but, when done properly, it is a great personal branding tool to get the word out on who you are and what makes you different from everyone else.

If doing this yourself seems tedious, remember that there are services and software out there that can do social media posting for you.

CHAPTER 11

STRATEGY 8 – BUILD YOUR PERSONAL BRAND WITH TWITTER

Personal branding is all about perception and what people are going to associate with you. Nowadays, with the emergence of social media platforms, people prefer to connect with other people rather than with a corporate brand. Branding is a way to make yourself memorable, whether you are an individual or a company.

When it comes to personal branding on Twitter, there are some things you should keep in mind.

1. Listen to the online conversation and participate - you will be able to use tools like Twitter search to distinguish between the "signal and the noise". By finding out what the "signals" are, you will find opportunities to engage in the conversations. Another way for companies to encourage participation in this new communication medium is to use Twitter to hold

contests.

2. Your content shapes your brand - what you choose to tweet will shape your brand on Twitter. Be aware that once you tweet, your content will be out there for people to find forever.

3. Build a community - just like Mr. Kutcher who found an audience that is interested in what he had to offer through his tweets. The chances are, your market is already out there on Twitter - by building an online presence, you will be able to engage with your niche market.

4. Always look to expand your visibility - you will be able to expand your visibility if you make a conscious effort to make yourself visible to the right group of people and influencers. Twitter is only one channel of social media, tools like LookupPage and Google Profiles can further your audience reach and visibility.

5. Build and nurture relationships - as a broadcasting tool, Twitter is great when it comes to reaching thousands of people in one swoop. It also makes you and your brand more reachable. Engage and respond to tweets directed at you, ask questions and answer them.

Twitter is not the only tool that can assist your personal branding efforts - there are various other channels that can help you establish and monitor your online brand identity.

By enhancing your personal branding efforts with tools such as LookupPage and Twitter, you will gain a competitive advantage over others who offer similar services and encourage more people to talk about you.

CHAPTER 12

STRATEGY 9 - BUILD YOUR PERSONAL BRAND BY MASTERING CONSISTENCY

Consistency offers many rewards to the entrepreneur and his business. It helps sharpen your business skills, grow your business and build your brand.

Running an internet business, especially on a shoestring budget, can easily leave you frustrated and unmotivated due to insignificant initial results. This phase of discouragement can totally ruin your business if you are ignorant of the importance of consistency in business.

Every bit of what you do with your internet business requires that you persist and do even more work. Just a little more and a little more. Eventually, you will get to that point where the little bit more effort you put in, becomes the drop that causes the spill. You will have reached the tipping point.

When I was preparing my first multifaceted internet marketing product, I would have many things in my journal to work on about the product every day. So daily, I would do some of those things and continue the next day, and the next day, etc.

It got to a point where I had finished every major thing I was supposed to do. This was surprising, as I would go through the journal repeatedly believing there would be something I had not done. I couldn't find anything. It was a wonderful feeling.

My point is that your business is like trying to push a heavy cart uphill. Though it may be difficult, every step you take moves that cart ever higher, and your business, from a lower level to a slightly higher one until you make that one last move - the tipping point move.

Being consistent requires dedication, commitment and discipline and requires that you set a goal and pursue it. No matter how small that action is, work on your business every day. This may sound obvious and may not need extra effort to convince you that it's important. I have believed in this idea for a long time but I have not been practicing it for that long.

There are other impacts consistency can have on your business more that I can cover here, but for the sake of this chapter, I'll discuss two.

1. Presentation Skill

Like anything you do consistently, your presentation skill will improve over time. As you persist you will find your thoughts become better organized and you expressions clearer.

Take Steve Jobs for example. If you watch his presentation video of twenty years ago which is available on YouTube, you'll see how he has improved over the decades. Steve Jobs in 1984 was charming but he was even more refined in 1997. The Steve Jobs that introduced the iPhone in 2007 was even better again.

When great ad writers like Drayton Bird, Clayton Makepeace and John Carlton look back on their old copies, while it was their best when they turned it out, they see a thousand ways they could have improved on them.

You don't buy experience; you get it by doing.

If you avoid doing your own presentations, you

become an expert at sourcing and managing people who do things for you - and that too is valuable. However, when you do your own presentations, when you write your own copy, you become an expert in presenting your ideas and products to the market.

This is priceless because no other person can really present your products with the enthusiasm you have. It's your product, you created it, you've seen it grow from inception and you, like no other person, know how it can change the lives of users.

2. Branding

You build a brand by consistent use of the things you want people to know you for.

You can do this in many ways.

Your Unique Selling Proposition (USP) is one way you build a brand; your core myth is another, and there are other ways too.

We have all become familiar with brands like NIKE because of the consistent use of the check mark and the 'Just do it' phrase, and Johnny Walker and the 'Keep walking' phrase because they use it so often. We got to know the Steve Job story and the core myth behind the Apple brand of computers because of the consistent telling of the story.

The relevance of consistency to a business sounds obvious, but in truth, it's more difficult to be okay consistent than it is to admit its importance.

CHAPTER 13

STRATEGY 10 – BUILD YOUR PERSONAL BRAND WITH FACEBOOK

Facebook has fast become the ultimate social media website for promoting businesses. Of course, Twitter and LinkedIn are also essential tools to use for networking but no one can deny the huge impact Facebook is having.

More businesses are getting on the bandwagon and actively participating on Facebook every day. Because of the demand, Facebook is also evolving to include tools and features that allow businesses to promote their services and products. It is important at this point to say that there is a proper process of marketing online effectively through using Facebook.

Below are 5 ways that you can use to build your brand on Facebook:

1. What Does Your Profile Say About You?

Set up your profile so that it helps to promote your business in a positive way. What is it that your business specializes in that will make it stand out from the crowd? What value do you bring to the community or network? This is your Unique Selling Proposition (USP) that will make people remember you.

Your profile should provide various links to your other web pages that you are associated with. If you have a personal website, such as a blog, it would be advantageous to add this so that people who are interested in you will go to your personal page to find out more about you.

Social etiquette is very important on the Facebook network. In no way do you want you or your business to come across as "spammy" by consistently posting links to your business products or services. This really does turn people off and your company can get a bad name.

Try and look at Facebook as being a "social network." That indeed is what it was created for. People go onto Facebook to unwind… a bit like going to the pub or bar after work and chilling out with your colleagues and friends. Last thing you want is to be constantly harassed with business after a hard day's work.

2. Find Your Key Target Audience

Finding your key target audience is integral in marketing. You want to be able to get your message across and ultimately sell to your target market audience. On Facebook, find niche related groups that are most relevant to your business. Become an active member by joining those groups.

Now you will be able to contribute to the groups by adding relevant high value content and in turn you will be building your own business branding in the process. On your profile page, be sure to include a personalized message when adding friends so that you can establish an "early" connection with the person.

When adding friends, you want to be able to engage and interact as quickly as you can. Find out more about them and the cardinal rule is not to come across as all "spammy" by thrusting your business products and services down their throats as soon as you have met them.

In fact you may hardly ever directly promote your products or services to your new "friends" or group members but they will get a chance to check out what you do by visiting your profile page or fan page through curiosity.

3. Add Value To Your Network

To set you apart as a leader, you need to provide high quality value to your network and share information from other content sites. You could provide valuable content from links to free training videos, eBooks, or affiliated sites which provides real valuable information.

Update your network regularly with your Facebook status, notes and posts. Creating unique content which you can share with the community would be a superb strategy and brand you as a market leader.

4. Get Leads From Another Sales Funnel.

You may have a lead capture page or content website like a blog which you use as your entry point for your marketing funnel. These are the 2 main ways that you can get prospective clients to opt in to your website and leave their name and email address.

Once you have this information, then you will be able to commence an email marketing campaign to direct your prospective clients to your business products and services.

This is a good point to direct them also to your Facebook fan page in particular and get your customers to engage and interact with you through there.

This can be very useful because it will give the prospective new client an opportunity to find out more about your company and the key members within the organization. Putting a face to names with photos and videos can really help to break the ice and make your clients see you and your business as being "real" and approachable.

5. Create a Fan Page and Group

You can also promote your business in many ways by creating a fan page and group. The Facebook fan page is fast becoming an integral part of marketing online for many businesses. How many "likes" you or your business have is proving to be the common denominator for how effectively you are branding your business online using Facebook.

There are many ways to promote your fan page and the one where I have seen personal success is through using Facebook Adverts. Facebook Adverts allows you to post a content ad onto Facebook and every time someone clicks on your ad or your ad is seen in terms of impressions, you will be charged accordingly.

This is also a highly effective way to market and you can direct your Facebook Ads to certain places on your fan page such as your blog, videos, built-in lead capture page, or a relevant article thread that you have created with other members through the comments that have been posted.

CHAPTER 14

STRATEGY 11 – BUILD YOUR PERSONAL BRAND WITH BOOK PUBLISHING

Writing and publishing your book is also very much about enhancing your personal brand tool in the market and we can adopt the same steps. In this chapter, the steps to creating a winning brand are summarized as 3 Es: Extract, Express and Exude. We can adopt the 3 steps to book publishing as follows:

Extract Phase

In the Extract Phase, it is essentially about extracting your brand essence that you wish to portray and put in your book. Before you can do that, you need to think hard about who you are and what makes you unique.

When you managed to unearth your unique promise of value, then you will be able to start conceptualizing the book idea and creating the book content that will enhance the personal brand that you are building.

In this phase, you should first identify and write down your purpose for publishing, your unique differentiation, competitive books and also how you will reach out to your target readers.

The output from the Extract Phase would look something like a publishing proposal and of course your completed manuscript. With that in hand, you are ready to move to the Express Phase where you develop and execute the communication and marketing plan.

Express Phase

The Express Phase is about identifying marketing channels and communication tools to reach your target reader effectively. A book is a powerful tool for you stand out from competition because it helps you to build visibility and credibility.

But this is only possible if the book reaches the hands of your target reader. A published book that sits in your storeroom collecting dust will never help to enhance your personal brand.

Having identified your target reader profile, you evaluate communication tools that can help you generate awareness for your book. Other than readers, your book needs to be in the hands of people who will be instrumental in expanding your success.

You have to research, identify and prioritize both offline and online means that can help you maximize the impact. This could be through news coverage, books reviews, author interviews, contribution of book blog etc.

An effective marketing plan must complement an effective communications plan because the last thing you want is that interested readers could not obtain a copy of your book. The marketing plan will identify channels that you can make your book available and remember that bookstore is only one of the channels.

It is not uncommon to come across authors who sell more copies of their book through their alternate channels than through bookstores. Other than just a physical book, you can also explore other means to express the book like audio book, e-book, etc. that can help you maximize the outreach from the same contents.

The output from the Express Phase is a comprehensive Book Communications and Marketing

Plan that you can execute. You are then ready to move on to the third and final phase, Exude.

Exude Phase

In the Express Phase, you developed a strategy for making your book visible to those who need to know about you so that you can achieve your goals. In this final Exude Phase, it is really about living your brand. You will align everything that surrounds you with your branding. This environment includes your social and professional network.

So whether you are giving a talk, conducting a workshop, granting an interview, networking or participating in social media, you should ensure that all activities are supporting your personal Brand and you leverage on your book as the branding tool.

To summarize, a published book is an effective tool that can help you to enhance your personal branding. To maximize the impact, you can adopt the 3-E process of Extract, Express and finally Exude to reinforce your unique promise of value through the book.

CHAPTER 15

STRATEGY 12 - BUILD YOUR PERSONAL BRAND WITH PERSEVEARNCE

The difference between those who make and those who don't is contained in a single idea: Perseverance. How can you achieve perseverance in the face of struggle and obstacles?

Make managing your energy the #1 priority.

If you focus on struggle and downfall, you'll very likely fail. But positive focus on your intentions produces the best outcomes. Athletes know this. That is why the mental game is more important than the physical.

HERE ARE THREE TIPS FOR MANAGING YOUR ENERGY:

1) Find awareness. It's almost impossible to manage your energy if you're not aware of what you're thinking and feeling.

- Analyze your thoughts from outside yourself.

Start to recognize your personal thoughts by separating yourself from your inner self and be rational about what you notice yourself thinking.

- Especially notice thoughts that are distracting you from the core values list that defines you. Noticing the things that detract from your goals is the first step to perseverance.

2) Understand how to feel good. If I wake up on the wrong side of the bed, I know I probably won't do good work unless I get myself out of my bad mood. Then I usually go for a run or do yoga. You can go for a walk, read affirmations, talk yourself out of it: find what works for you to snap out of it.

- The foundation of feeling good is building up your self-esteem. The best way to develop lasting self-esteem is by being accountable to yourself with a mental core values list that keeps your personal integrity. The more integrity you have in your life, the more you trust yourself and the better you feel.
- Always mean and keep the promises you make to yourself. The worst hits to my self-esteem were not the promises I broke to others, but the

ones I didn't keep to myself. Just like the best business brands make and keep promises to their customers, your self-esteem will come from the personal promises you keep. That's what makes branding personal.

3) Commit to a way of being. You don't need a world-changing vision to inspire perseverance. It can simply be about choosing to live your core values list and making people feel your personal integrity.

People always remember how you make them feel more than anything else.

If you value kindness, then your reason for being reliable and consistent with other people isn't dictated by external circumstances. Your drive comes from inside you-your Brand from Within. That's just what perseverance is made of: consistently knowing who you are and what you're working for and striving towards it with the right energy and best intentions.

CHAPTER 16

STRATEGY 13 – BUILD YOUR PERSONAL BRAND WITH INTEGRITY

Building a brand is not a gimmick or fluke, marketing for deep positive branding is a necessary part of business. If marketing with integrity is at the core of your business, you can develop branding strategies that are customer focused built on your values.

A major aspect of branding for any business is the customer's experience from first learning about the company to actually using the product. Competitive pricing, quality return policy and programs to generate customer loyalty all add up to effective customer service.

Running a business with integrity includes asking for customer feedback, efficiently handing customer complaints and truth in advertising, your brand's essence is based on the promises made with the initial branding. From the onset, give your potential customers your brand's promise in the simplest terms possible then live up that promise, that is customer service.

Consistent visual branding

Visual branding is very powerful. Both online and offline branding is built on your use of logos, banners, tag lines, packaging, business cards, advertising and direct marketing tools. Even if funds are limited, you can strive to be consistent and creative with your visual branding efforts.

As your business grows, invest in creating a visual logo that can be built into all aspects of your business. Remember that your brand's promise and personality is most effective if your customers can mentally connect your logo with your business.

The use of a trademark is an integral part long term visual branding. A trademark also protects your business in the long run. Building your brand with a trademark occurs when you convey you are a serious contender for their business.

When your potential customer is on the fence between two companies seemingly equal companies, a trademark can influence their choice. Your customer service from sale to repeat sale will help keep them loyal customers but getting that initial foothold will either make or break your business.

Branding through relationships with your customers.

Through building relationships with your visitors and customers, you will create deep connections that compel them to return to you for future business.

Granted many customers buy based on price or brand names regardless of the environment or customer relations but if your business is built on customers rather than sales, you will learn the power of branding through relationships.

Essentially, it comes down to what your business offers. A service business can only thrive when you are able to develop strong professional relationships with your customers. If you run a website that offers digital products with little human interaction then you may discount the relationship aspect. Smart business? I don't think so.

Customer loyalty and word of mouth recommendations come from customers impressed with your product, service and the way they were treated by you and your team. That's the bottom line. The long term benefit of connecting with your customers definitely outweighs any short team business success.

Personality branding lifts a business apart from the competition and above similar business with the human element of the business. Your brand's "personality" is made up of the human aspect of your brand.

Think of the customers you seek. Consider the human traits that will draw them toward your brand. Does your brand project warmth, fun, wit, efficiency, imagination, maturity or thriftiness?

The human elements you convey in your marketing and branding will be key to reaching your target market. Investment bankers often use branding strategies that convey steady, mature, serious and bottom line thinking because those are what their potential customers seek.

CHAPTER 17

STRATEGY 14 – BUILD YOUR PERSONAL BRAND WITH CREDIBILITY

The concept of creating a brand out of your business, or even yourself, has become the ultimate strategy in marketing and globalizing your product or service. Branding, however, cannot occur without credibility. Enhance your personal credibility, and watch your business soar. Here are some simple tips to increase your personal credibility ratings.

Walk the Talk. Always deliver, and if possible, OVER-deliver on your promises. Nothing will harm your personal credibility more than saying one thing, and then doing another. Make it your aim to lead by example, not words.

Always Keep Your Appointments. Being late for meetings (for those working from home, a scheduled phone call is considered a meeting.) or constantly rescheduling them, not calling after you promised you would, or in any other way failing to meet deadlines, is the easiest way to kill your business.

People will take your lack of punctuality to mean a lack of professionalism and interest. Nobody will be willing to follow, buy from, or partner with someone who does not care enough about their business to be on time.

Don't be a "Know-it-all". People are not interested in doing business with someone who has all the answers. They ARE, however, very interested in the leadership of someone who is honest and willing to find new answers and solutions.

If you don't know an answer admit it, but offer to find it. Never brainstorm aloud before customers or employees, unless you are in the middle of a brainstorming session. People will often mistake your ramblings to be real proposals or responses to issues being discussed. Think before you speak.

Under Promise, and Over Deliver. If you have a new contract that you think will take you three weeks to complete, offer to deliver it in four. If the client considers four weeks to be a reasonable amount of time to complete the project, they will be highly impressed, and a lot more likely to offer you other contracts, once you deliver the completed work a week early.

On the contrary, if you sing your own praises and sell yourself as the ultimate in what you do, but then run into unexpected snags, the client will more than likely think twice about hiring you, let alone referring you to others.

Know Your Limits. Don't take on more than you can effectively do. If you already have a project that will consume all your energy and resources for the next couple of weeks, don't take on anything else for that period of time.

No one will think less of you for knowing your limits; on the contrary, they will respect you for it. If, however, you choose to overextend yourself, and deliver mediocre work, they will take that to be the true quality of your work. Give yourself the opportunity to keep all your commitments with excellence.

Branding is not a mystical force that is only granted by the powers that be to the chosen few. Enhancing your personal credibility within the business arena, will help your name be known and branded as people continue to spread the word on your high-quality work. Work on yourself more than you do your business, and the rest will fall into place.

CHAPTER 18

STRATEGY 15 – BUILD YOUR PERSONAL BRAND WITH CUSTOM PROMOTIONAL PRODUCT

If you are looking for a good way to build a strong relationship with your customers, custom promotional products may be your answer. A custom product says more than just a small pencil with your company's logo on it.

A custom product can say that you care about the customer more than other products will. These gifts can be more unique as well. When a person gets one of these products they will feel that they have received something very special, not just some mass produced item for advertising.

They will feel that they have attained a gift that is specially meant for them and they will find a unique use for your custom promotional products to fit their needs as well. They will use the item often and they will want to brag to their friends and family about how they got this great gift because they are such a loyal customer of your company.

Not only will they be spreading the word about their own abundance, but they will be spreading the word about how your company is a great company that makes people happy with quality products and a quality service that is worth going to time and time again.

By showing the world that you are worth doing business with on many occasions, you show the world that the first time they do business with you will be an enjoyable experience.

These custom promotional products are good for building strong relationships with clients because they present the attitude of your company more accurately than just a logo.

The logo will be presented as well, but the product will also gain a significant amount of attention which gives the logo even more prestige. These types of free gifts also come in a wide variety of options. You can choose from very unique items that other companies might not consider offering.

This will give your company an edge because the customers will associate your company with leading edge ideas. The customer will know that you care more about them then just giving a simple giveaway. You offer a custom give away that in many ways will be perceived as a gift that is just for them.

Custom promotional products can be very beneficial to gaining a good attitude offered towards your company. Clients will be very grateful to get an interesting item for free and they will get a good amount of use out of the product which can only benefit your company.

The more a client wants to use the gift that you give them, the better the chances are that they will spread the word to a great deal of people.

Simple discounted custom promotional products can easily become a very effective advertising campaign. The person may take a custom printed bag that you gave them half way around the world.

Then the exposure your company and the logo printed will be gaining widespread popularity. The more popular your logo and slogan become, the more popular your company becomes. This is a great reason to get one of the many custom products available today.

CHAPTER 19

STRATEGY 16 – BUILD YOUR PERSONAL BRAND WITH YOUTUBE CHANNEL

Branding yourself with the YouTube channel is like having your own show. The first thing you need to look at is: "Are you choosing to brand yourself or your company?"

After you have decided which brand you want to market for, you will need to create a custom design background for your YouTube channel. You need to start thinking of branding your own image because, by doing so, you will be standing out from your competitors.

This will position yourself powerfully in your market. Having your own image logo to brand yourself with YouTube channel can be a very powerful tool to your business and get people's attention.

Just think about those big companies like HP, Apple, Microsoft, etc. that are making millions of dollars that have done the same thing - brand yourself for your credibility and awareness.

Why custom design background is important? Because image is the key and drives more traffic to your website. Most importantly, you will become the expert in your niche if you know how to imprint your own logo image into people's mind.

Just imagine when you go to visit someone's YouTube channel and it looks really plain, would you think this page looks really different or just like everyone else's? Does it bring out your curiosity?

On the other hand, 98% of people are attracted to visual images and when you see someone's page looks nicely done with his/her custom design background, would it make you stay a bit longer and curious to find out what this person does? Would you be wondering how much time and effort this person has spent on his/her design image background?

A simple secret is to start by branding yourself with YouTube channel by building your own custom design background if you want to focus on video marketing.

Our main focus is to attract 20% of highly qualified

leads to your business so you will always attract to the right type of clients. By doing so, you can pre-qualify your prospects quickly, you create a trust-known factor, and you build an interest and customer loyalty.

So how to create an custom design background image within your niche that is going to make you stand out?

I have personally used 99design.com for my logo design. 99design.com is a marketplace by a massive community of designers and contest holders. Designer then compete their peers in design contests to win prizes offered by the contest holders, improve their skills and establish relationships with new clients.

All you need to do is provide the information you would like to have your logo designed. You can then pick and choose which design you like the best out of those designers in your contest. It's really simple and fun to get your logo done.

You can also visit tweetpages.com for more custom design backgrounds. They offer all sorts of background designs with affordable rate to fit in your budget, for both twitter and YouTube channel.

Again, having your custom design background can brand yourself with YouTube channel to make it look approachable and fun. It's all about being creative and stand out of your competition. If your website or videos are not driving as much traffic as you want it to be, it might be a good opportunity to update your custom design background.

CHAPTER 20

STRATEGY 17 – BUILD YOUR PERSONAL BRAND WITH JOINT VENTURE

Joint venture (JV's) can be a gold mine. They can turn your business around. Working with a superstar partner will build your brand because some of his or her superstar credibility ("street cred") rubs off on you. You can gain access to audiences faster than doing almost anything else.

On the other hand, JVs can be a huge waste of time, leaving you with no money, lost time and a former partner who prints out your home page and throws darts at it.

Here are the three hot button questions you need to answer.

Is this JV a strong fit for your brand?

Not every partner will build your business. Some will actually detract from your mission. If you're a down-to-earth, no-nonsense type, your followers will be puzzled when you introduce someone who reads tarot cards to find her destiny,

Your choice will be influenced by more than topic. What does your potential partner offer by way of promotion? I won't partner with anyone who has a weak sales letter or who makes promises that I suspect are not realistic.

What do you bring to the table?

A joint venture is just that - joint. That means each partner has something to bring to the table. Do you have a big list? A product with a proven, tested sales page? A reputation as the go-to person in your niche so your light will shine on your new partner?

Are you taking the initiative to invite a JV partner? Then you're selling yourself as an opportunity. Any prospective partner worth seeking has options. Everybody sells even the 5-star, gilt-edged, platinum-coated gurus. If you don't know how to write a JV invitation, hire a copywriter or marketing coach. My Espresso Consultation was designed for this type of project.

Are you completely free from need or greed?

Approach your JV partner in the spirit of abundance. Recently someone asked me, "Can I invite someone to create a campaign for me in return for a share of the proceeds?" Even if you could, that's rarely a good idea.

When you get confident answers to these three questions, you will be well on your way to your own joint venture success.

CHAPTER 21

STRATEGY 18 – BUILD YOUR PERSONAL BRAND WITH WEB DESIGN

One of the most important aspects of getting your name out there is brand building, which most people achieve with business cards, brochures, television advertisements, radio jingles and newspaper or magazine spreads.

Did you know, however, that one of the best ways to build your brand is through your website? If you are wondering what changes you can make to your web design to make sure it promotes your brand in the best way possible, you should utilize the following tips:

Color - The color palette that you choose for your web design is very important, not just for the aesthetics of the site but also for the emotions and associations that each color carries. The color red, for example, symbolizes passion, energy, power and excitement, which is why it is often chosen by brands in the entertainment industry.

Character - You could try to infuse your brand with some personality to really help you to define what you stand for. You should shape your brand's character around something that you think your audience would associate themselves with - are you all about safety and reliability, or are you more about fun and being down to earth?

Emotion - Another thing that your web design should include is emotion - what feelings and emotions do you want your visitors to experience? When putting your website together, you shouldn't be focusing on following the latest design trends - you should be focusing on the emotions and ideas that you want your brand to project.

Consistency - The foundations of a successful brand are that it will be memorable. So, how do you make people remember something? You repeat it over and over. By having a certain consistency throughout your website, you can not only build on the personality that you worked on earlier, you can also ensure that the site presents a uniform image.

Tone - You should also take into account the language and tone of voice that is invoked through the content of your web design, as this needs to reinforce your brand's personality. You might use an informal and fun tone for a down to earth website for tech savvy youngsters, or a formal and intellectual tone for a serious business website for professionals.

There are, of course, plenty of other ways that you could work to build your brand through your web design - including the reuse of code and visuals, the size and position of your logo, value proposition, and the uniqueness of the website as a whole but the five outlined above tend to be the most valuable.

If you have been looking for new ways to build your brand and get your name out there, your website should be the first place you look.

CHAPTER 22

STRATEGY 19 - BUILD YOUR PERSONAL BRAND WITH PHOTO KEY RINGS

A business man cannot stop with manufacturing the product and sending it to his dealers for sale. He has to initiate steps and work out strategies to make the product familiar and popular amongst consumers. Giving away promotional gift items is one of such strategies adopted by any business person.

The Commonest yet cost effective promotional tool popular in the business arena is key ring. Because key rings and chains are used by one and all over and over in day to day life it will be ideal gift that can be given by corporate people and individual business man.

However, giving away keys rings in an attractive shape with the corporate message on them may sometimes does not result in the expected brand promotion. It requires something extra, something that will bring smile and cheer on the face of the user -

personalization.

A small provision attached to the key ring like tiny photo frame with the photo of the customer or any attractive picture will make the key ring more attractive and enhance its promotional value.

Photo key rings seem to be the best solution because:

They have a great degree of personalization

An emotional quotient is attached to them

People love seeing their pictures and photos of their beloved ones

Photo key rings can be given to the employees also, because:

Morale of the employee is boosted

Employee is proud of the company that he is working for

Company gets recognition since the name and company logo is present

Product gets advertised since many people see the key ring when the employee is using it

It would act as a motivational factor which will increase the productivity of the employee.

Moreover, these key rings will not pinch the budget and will bring the desired result.

CHAPTER 23

STRATEGY 20 – BUILD YOUR PERSONAL BRAND WITH BRAND BOOK

A brand book is a set of rules and guidelines for the use of your brand. A standard if you must. A style guide, in a designer's context. It basically explains how to properly make use of elements to make sure that it is consistent with your brand.

Having a brand book makes it easier to do a project. Example: if you decided to do a packaging for a brand product, presenting the brand book to the designer would make things easier to select font styles, colors, and whatnot and output would be consistent with your brand.

Makes you look professional. Being consistent with your marketing tools and outputs makes you look professional. Like everything's planned out to be the way they are. You will have control of your brand. Having standardized brand gives your control of any loose ends. If something is not working - a look or feel

- you refer to your trusty old brand book.

Never a cheap moment. When you have a brand that's solid in all corners, your brand would avoid looking cheap. You enhance your brand. With your brand's style regulated, it makes you progress into a finer and solid brand. You are put onto a perspective where you see your brand's untapped potential and develop changes for its betterment.

What to Include in a Brand Book?

There are several components to include in a brand book. Here are the basics and must be included.

BRAND OVERVIEW

As much as possible, this should be brief. In little words as possible, make sure that the concept for the design of your brand is clear. A designer should likely read this very important part of the brand book; it should tell what the brand is aiming to be, its look and feel.

LOGOS

A logo is the brand's key component to its strategy; therefore, it should be taken seriously. The brand will likely revolve around the logo concept BUT the logo is not your brand alone. Make sure there are many logo variations for certain styles and backgrounds, and clarify minimum sizes.

INCORRECT LOGO USAGE

Remember when I said, a detail can make or break your brand? Here's a common mistake in the branding world: logos are used and stamped upon on almost anything.

Your brand has to look professional, and you should know not to mess around with it. If you do, you're basically messing with your reputation. You have to be careful to make sure that designers or anyone that would make use of your brand logo understands what they can and cannot do with it.

FONTS

Font is crucial. It also affects your brand's feel. You have to define what kind of typefaces to use. More so, their size, colors, headline and body typeface. Do not forget to include web and non-web fonts.

COLORS

Since your brand revolves around your logo, and your logo revolves around a particular color set, it is imperative to make sure that the use of colors is specified. Specify primary and secondary colors - when and where to use them. Include color palettes, as well as, formats for both print and web end.

COPY AND TONE OF VOICE

Think of this as another key component to your brands personality. It's how you would want them to "hear" or "read" you - your character. Defining the way you deal or sound like, especially in the social media, is a great way to be consistent. When there are several people writing or doing the copy in their different ways, your brand would seem to have several personalities. That is why it is key to have these laid out properly.

ICONOGRAPHY

Specify what size, spacing, and where to use icons is significant to promote consistency.

OTHER COMPONENTS THAT CAN BE INCLUDED

There are still several components that you can integrate in your brand book. It's really up to you and up to the industry your business is in. Some components that you could consider include:

- Photography style

- Supporting graphic elements

- Design layouts and grids

- Social media profile page applications

- Brochure/flyer layout options

- Website layout

- Signage specifications

- Advertising treatments

- Merchandising applications

Who makes a Brand Book?

Usually, brand books are developed by an experienced graphic designer. Sometimes, the agency where your logo is made could do this for you. Even if you already have a logo, you can always hire someone to make your brand book. But of course, it's better to have the one who made your logo do the brand book for you, as well, to ensure that it flows well with your logo. It is always better to have a PDF format brand book for you, aside from it being printed. It'll make things convenient especially during a project where you can always send it via email.

The Bottom Line

Your logo is a significant component of your brand. Several aspects of your business revolve around it, especially in the modern branding world. But your logo alone is not your brand.

It's just a part of your strategy to be identified with. How your logo is treated and used is where your branding unfolds. By having a brand book, you can ensure that everything works consistently to have a strong and solid brand.

CHAPTER 24

STRATEGY 21 – A BUILD YOUR PERSONAL BRAND WITH AFFILIATE MARKETING

Personal Branding means building up your presence as an expert on subjects related to what you're selling or on the art of Affiliate Marketing (depending on your target market).

You then build relationships with your potential customers/list and promote yourself and your understanding to help others, rather than marketing your Affiliate products/services upfront.

The idea is that customers will grow to know, like, trust and respect you - and thus will come to want to buy what you are selling because they trust your solutions to their problems.

You can add value by offering information, expertize, solutions, empathy and understanding to your target market - via personal contact (emails) and your individualized websites/blogs.

Choose the products/services you will be promoting carefully - and around a theme, so that your potential customers are offered a full range of everything they need (and you get to gain because customers will often buy something else related to what they've just bought, if you sell it too).

What does this mean for Affiliate Marketers?

It means preferably don't use the standard template Affiliate Company websites/lead capture pages and pre-prepared autoresponder emails; or if these are working for you to some degree, then supplement these with personalized contact with your list, to build strong relationships with these potential customers.

It also means more work. Work on building relationships with your list, work on increasing your knowledge and expertise and sharing it with others, work on creating a personalized space on the Internet where you can showcase your uniqueness and your ability to help others - via your own website or blog.

Make sure you're promoting quality products and

services that really do work in the way promised to your customers, and market these in a way that fits with your personality. This means your list will get to know you, perceive how you are different from other marketers, and sense how valuable you are to them in a multitude of ways.

Ultimately, all of this should mean more money for you, the Affiliate Marketer. Maybe not as quickly as you hope, because building up a unique online presence, growing a list of potential customers, and becoming known, liked and respected, all takes time.

But there are Affiliate Marketers out there, who experienced a 'eureka' moment, where after a lot of hard work, it all started happening very quickly for them. The common denominator for most of them was their personalized marketing and relationship building, and that their customers had got to know and like them over time.

CHAPTER 25

TIPS FOR A SUCCESSFUL PERSONAL BRANDING STRATEGY

A personal brand is all about getting noticed, or standing out in the crowd by displaying unique talents and attributes. Personal branding should not be just limited to projecting an image, but the focus should be on projecting the right image.

The main idea to conceptualize while working upon personal branding strategies is to decide what should be enhanced and projected. Following are a few tips to get you started.

Strength and Weakness: Before beginning the process of personal branding, it is important to understand yourself well. Your talents, attributes, interests, goals, dreams, passions, vision, area of specialization, weakness, etc. should be clear to you. Find your niche.

Creating and Owning the Brand: You, as a brand should be perceived by others as you want them to, and not the other way around. Define your path clearly. The brand you create should be strong, reliable and consistent. A wavering self-image can become very damaging.

Brand Visualization: Unless you are seen, you won't be recognized or remembered, and at the same time too much of you will prove to be saturating. Be seen and heard at the right places. Tools such as business cards, portfolio, blogs, websites, forums, Facebook, etc., will speak volumes about your vision.

Focus on Building a Personal Brand: Getting started is usually easy. Staying focused and true to your vision is an important aspect of personal branding. Adaptability to changes should be done in a manner that does not detract you from your goal. It should rather become a process to achieve your goals.

Target Audience: While building a personal brand, it is important to understand who your audience is. To understand the target audience and how you wish to be perceived by them, understand what you are; are you an employer, employee, manager, owner, etc.?

Personal branding strategy also includes overcoming barriers such as gender, cultural, educational, etc. By being true to yourself, playing to your strengths and practicing excellence you will be easily able to create a successful personal brand.

The concept of "branding yourself" was once used predominantly in the marketing industry. Today, however, with the growth and development of technology that enables anyone access to the Internet, personal branding is no longer reserved just for those who have the assets to pay for an expensive marking strategy.

Anyone can use multiple media platforms to get their brand out into the marketplace: Twitter, Facebook, blogging, and LinkedIn.

The concept of "branding yourself" was once used predominantly in the marketing industry. Today, however, with the growth and development of technology that enables anyone access to the Internet, personal branding is no longer reserved just for those who have the assets to pay for an expensive marking strategy.

Anyone can use multiple media platforms to get their brand out into the marketplace: Twitter, Facebook, blogging, and LinkedIn.

If you were to ask 50 people to define personal branding, each would likely give you a different answer. For the purpose of this lesson, however, we will define branding yourself as promoting your unique identity.

We equate self-promotion with branding because branding is what you are doing when you develop your personal assets, personality, and passion through online and in-person marketing.

With branding, you promote yourself to attract even more opportunities to talk about yourself to others. You find opportunities to tell your story, give your pitch, and let people see what makes you special.

The two things that you will need to be especially passionate about are who you are and the work you do. You must build a personal brand that evokes feelings of well-established brands such as Starbucks, McDonalds, Facebook, and Google.

Knowing yourself helps you to create your personal brand, to be able to state what sets you apart from others, and to identify what gives you motivation and drive. It will provide you with the confidence to get out there and sell yourself to the industry, and, specifically, to the positions that you aspire to.

This confidence will spring from your competency about your unique product (you). When you are confident in your skills and assets, others will feel more confident about selecting you for that position.

Now that you have uncovered what you like, we can accurately market your services to the right companies the offer the right work environments for you.

It is smart to build and sustain a meaningful network through the effective use of both online and in-person networking tools and opportunities. Through this process, you can build your reputation and create networks with unprecedented reach.

Your goal should be to authentically share your own qualities and passion about what you love to do. This authenticity will come through as you develop your brand identity.

Developing your brand and standing apart from the crowd is critical in this changing employment environment where technical workers are often more knowledgeable about their field than their CEOs or leaders are.

It is therefore important that you discover ways to define the key value that you bring to corporations and to develop strategies to communicate this value personally both within and across organizations to manage your brand effectively over time.

Defining your brand is the first step in developing a sales and marketing plan for your defining qualities. You may be quick to say that you dislike selling-or even the idea of it-but we all have learned to sell from an early age.

As children we begin by selling our parents on things we want, such as staying up late, or going to a friend's house for the weekend, or the destination for our next family vacation.

This sales experience prepares you for life as a professional, during which you must sell your value, such as gaining entrance to a good school or college, acquiring the position that you desire, or getting a good deal on a house or car.

Once you get past the fear of selling, you will be able to focus on your strengths, communicate your value, and sell your brand to the world. The key to being effective in any role is the ability to influence how others perceive you.

Most buying decisions are based on trust and confidence in the product the consumer is buying, feelings that often inspire a sense of connection with a person or service.

Often, the trusted relationship is more important than the product's performance itself, and brands have become very powerful-especially with the changes in our technological environment.

We are bombarded with branded advertisements. It is commonly known by marketing experts that consumers are willing to pay up to 12 percent more for a brand that they feel they can trust and know than a new brand on the market.

CONCLUSION

Personal branding is not just for people who are in the public eye. Personal branding is for everyone and it is essential that you understand how important it is for you and for your business. That is especially true nowadays, with the popularity of the Internet and with the explosive amount of interactions on the various social media channels.

There are many important reasons why your personal brand is critical to your business's success. First of all, you need a personal brand because people are going to do searches and they are going to find you and your business (if you are lucky).

You absolutely want that to happen. In fact, if it doesn't happen in exactly that way, you will have no hope of building a relationship with them and eventually getting them to want to buy what you are selling (it is irrelevant whether it is a product, a service, or both).

The truth is that your online connections will be

looking for the best in that particular category and when they come upon your information, it may take a little while and a lot of evaluation before they decide to actually contact you. That is exactly why you need to make sure that your personal brand is in tip-top shape.

In the past, the way that you would have gone about creating a personal brand, developing that personal brand, and perfecting that personal brand was very different from it is today. In the past, you could make it a reality by simply declaring it to be the case.

At the time, your target audience probably didn't expect a great deal from you and your business so it was easy to establish your personal brand and to get other people to buy into it. You never really had to "put your money where your mouth was." In other words, you never actually had to prove that whatever you were saying was actually true.

It is a really good idea to take a good, hard look at your personal brand and to determine if it is what it needs to be at this point. If you come to the conclusion that it is lacking (by today's standards), you need to fix it as quickly as possible.

It is extremely important that you remember that your brand must be consistent across all of your communications (in every form). If your message is strong and consistent, other people will not have the power to say or do anything that is contrary to that.

In this day and age of technology, it is normal to expect that everyone who is considering connecting with you on a professional level will check you out before you ever actually speak with each other.

You need to be sure about what a search will uncover about you and your business. Leave nothing to chance, ever. It is critical that you know exactly what the searcher will find when that person searches for you.

If you aren't sure what the person will find and you are not exactly sure about what to do to ensure that the person finds exactly what you want that person to find, you can take the simple approach.

Make sure that all of your social media profiles are as complete as possible: You probably have profiles on Facebook, Twitter, LinkedIn, and the other popular social media channels on which other people are also interacting. That is great.

However, it is very important that your profiles on all of those social media channels are complete. How else do you expect other people to get to know you online. After all, that is why you have social media profiles. Your profiles are not for you. They are for other people.

Make sure that your LinkedIn profile is complete: LinkedIn is the most effective social media channel for professionals. If you aren't taking advantage of all that LinkedIn has to offer, it is definitely time to start doing so.

If a person searches for you on LinkedIn (and, trust me, they will), you want to be able to give them helpful, valuable information about you and your business.

There are many people who are visual and your content will make a much more positive impact if you balance the words on the paper with a graphic element as well. The bottom line is that you want your content to be noticed so that the people online start to interact with you and to build a relationship with you. Graphics will make your content pop and it will get noticed really well.

Your online connections will generally be more than happy to give you recommendations. Basically, all they have to do is to push a button. It is easy and it looks really good for you. There may be a debate as to whether recommendations actually have any effect either way but it can't hurt to have them.

This is something that other people will definitely be looking for when they search for you online. It is important to remember that you are the only person in the universe who can't express how amazing you and your business are.

The only people who have the credibility to do that are other people. Think about those testimonials as jewels. If you own beautiful jewels, it is unfair to keep them locked in a safe somewhere. You should share them with the world.

Your personal brand is your calling card in so many ways. It is a representation of who you are and of what you can do for other people.

Just like the other important elements of your business, it is important to visit your brand often and to make adjustments whenever you feel they are necessary. Also, bear in mind that your personal brand will make a lasting impression on other people.

So, make sure that it is everything that you want and need it to be. So, be creative, be inventive, be sensitive, and be compelling. It will work very well for you and your business.

Best wishes.

www.ingramcontent.com/pod-product-compliance
Lightning Source LLC
Chambersburg PA
CBHW071038240526
45469CB00006BD/2251